Charlotte's
Journey to
freedom

How to Build a Successful Business from
Scratch While Having a 9-5 Job

CAROLINA CANOSA-CRIADO

BALBOA.PRESS
A DIVISION OF HAY HOUSE

Balboa Press books may be ordered through booksellers or by contacting:

Balboa Press
A Division of Hay House
1663 Liberty Drive
Bloomington, IN 47403
www.balboapress.co.uk
UK TFN: 0800 0148647 (Toll Free inside the UK)
UK Local: (02) 0369 56325 (+44 20 3695 6325 from outside the UK)

Print information available on the last page.

ISBN: 978-1-6698-1502-0 (sc)
ISBN: 978-1-6698-1504-4 (hc)
ISBN: 978-1-6698-1503-7 (e)

Balboa Press rev. date: 11/22/2021

This book is dedicated to Sara and Victoria. Everything in life is possible if you believe in yourselves. Dreams are real.

CONTENTS

INTRODUCTION

Charlotte is a professional modern woman who had a "perfect" life. She was married with two children, and she had a successful professional career working for one of the biggest corporations at the City of London.

However, she was not happy, and there was something missing. She reached her fortieth birthday, and a series of events led her to leave her job and to start a difficult journey to entrepreneurship—something that had never crossed her mind before.

She knew that she did not want to spend the rest of her life in a job trading time for money whilst her children were growing. She always thought that there had to be other options to live in a comfortable way, with a balance between professional and personal life. She was very good in her job, but she felt that she was stuck, and upon looking at the future of her career, she knew that she would be in the same or slightly better position for years to come if she did not do anything about it now. Charlotte also knew that she did not want her income to be capped by an employer or her bosses, but she did not know how to move forward.

After a series of things happened to her, she decided to jump from her comfort zone and start her own business. She was not specially gifted in anything special, but she decided to try an online business even though she had no experience. Everything started smoothly, but there was something that nobody could foresee: It was the beginning of 2020, when the COVID-19 lockdown started in the United Kingdom. How could anyone survive when starting a business in the middle of that uncertainty? In addition, she was living in London and paying a mortgage, and like many middle-class Londoners, two people's salaries were needed to live in a comfortable way. Now that her job was gone and the pandemic had started, the only way she could survive was to try to continue with her business under those new conditions.

Would she manage to succeed? Would she give up? This story shows how a decision changed the lives of all the people around her for years to come, including her. It also shows how perseverance, hard work, and a positive mindset is needed to survive.

Charlotte's story could be your story. It could help you plan the steps and take action to get freedom without waiting until retirement, when it might be too late to enjoy life.

This book is based on a real-life story.

Enjoy it!

PART I

THE BEGINNING!

CHAPTER ONE

LIFE AS IT SHOULD BE

CHARLOTTE WOKE UP. It was 6.45 a.m. on Monday. She was going to work but did not want to wake up. She had the job that everyone would love, but there was something missing. She had a lovely husband and two daughters that were her life, and she had what she thought was the prefect job! But she knew that something was missing. She finally got up because in the end, it was just a new day. Her husband was a very busy lawyer, and they both had good jobs. They have an accommodating life. The kids were also ready for breakfast, and twenty minutes later, everyone was ready to leave the house for work and school. Charlotte was always late, and ran runs to take the tub. Her life was perfect, and she had a house in London. She paid the mortgage as many of her colleagues did. London was an exciting and expensive city, and both salaries were needed to have a comfortable life.

Charlotte had a lovely family and a lot of friends. She was

thirty-nine years old, and anyone would say that her life was perfect. Deep inside, she knew there was something missing. She was stuck in a nine-to-five job, and she realised that unless she did something different, she would be in that job and in the same position forever. She knew that her job was very stable; she was well paid, and nobody would fire her. However, she had been in the same position for the last five years. Every time she tried to move up to get a promotion, her boss said that she was not prepared. She was good enough to be in that position, and nobody knew how to perform it as well as she did. She wanted more. Across all the years she had worked for that company, she had seen all her colleagues move up—all except her. She was bored, and she had very limited possibilities to move up. However, according to some of her friends, she was privileged because she had an amazing job in a great company.

Charlotte did not see it the same way. She was stuck. However, deep inside, she knew she could do better outside. But how and where? She knew there was a world outside waiting for her, but she was afraid because she was paying for a mortgage, schools, and holidays. And what if it did not work? That fear was always there, and at the end of the day, there were not too many brave colleagues who decided to leave and adventure, going on to something better.

She did not know that the corporate world engages employees in a way that they think they are trapped and that after the corporate world, there is nothing.

Charlotte had had an idea going around her head for some months, but she was waiting for the right moment to put into practice her idea. She had always wanted to be an entrepreneur and have her own company. But all the stories around her told that it was not possible. Only the careless, single people without kids who had nothing to lose did it. She was not that kind of person. She would be crazy—and what would her colleagues and friends think about it? She realised that she had to do something crazy to get out of that very comfortable zone that was silently eating her up inside. Every day she saw all her colleagues as zombies, having nine-to-five jobs until they were old enough to get a "decent" pension, exchanging time and life for money. They were scared of changing something due to fear of not being successful and the shame of rejection when moving to another company or setting up their own businesses. That was not what "normal" people did. So many of her colleagues do nothing to change it for years and years.

One day, one of her colleagues, Andrew, a very nice colleague in his sixties who had been in that company for twenty-two years, left because finally he got his pension. Charlotte went to the farewell drinks, and during a conversation with her, he said some words that resonated deep inside her heart that made her change her mind. He said, "Do you know, Charlotte, I see you young with a beautiful family. And I can see myself as a mirror, and I made a great mistake. I thought that staying in my comfort zone and staying in this job until I retired would make my life easier, but it was not true. You can see all our colleagues around us, and they think they are in a good and safe position, doing nothing to change it because that is the easiest way. And they will probably end like I did.

"Now, I realise I have wasted at least fifteen years of my life being fearful of changing what I could change at that time. I had two young kids and a lovely partner, as you do right now. I could have taken the risk of moving to another company and getting a better salary, or creating my own business. Even if it did not work, it would be good to take the chance. Why not? In the end, I might have found a way of making it work. I might have succeeded. Now I am sixty-five years old, I have worked all my life, and I'm still healthy. And although I have a decent pension, I will never know what might have happened if I had jumped to the unknown and succeeded.

"I know I still have time, but it is not the same. I was in the same position and in the same job for fifteen years. I thought I would get a promotion year by year, but that was not true. I wrongly thought that if I worked hard, it would be recognised with a promotion. But it never happened, and I was too scared to act and start doing something else. Do not fall into the same trap. It's never going to be the perfect time to do it. It is now and here. The bosses I had during those fifteen years were always giving me compliments about how good I was, but they never gave me the chance to show that I could really do more than that.

"And here I am in my last day of my job, in the same position and almost with the same salary during the last fifteen years. During all those years, nothing happened. I am telling you this because I feel you are different and are a good person. Look around you: almost all your colleagues are like zombies, scared because they are unable to take risks. They will probably end up like me. They will spend their lives here wishing that someone is going to help them to move up. They do not know that they are the ones who can make it happen—not their bosses or someone else. I wish someone would have told me those words when I was your age."

It deeply shocked Charlotte. For a couple of weeks, she had those words in her head. She wanted to make sure she would not end up like the zombies around her. She spent a couple of weeks of looking at her kids walking at Richmond Park, wishing to have more time to enjoy her life, and knowing that if she did not do anything, she would never know if doing something different would change her life and the lives of her family. On that day, she decided to take a chance. She would not be another zombie. She decided to change it now and forever.

CHAPTER TWO

BEING BRAVE IS WHAT IT TAKES!

CHARLOTTE WAS FULL of fear about starting the new project she had been thinking of. Everyone thought she was crazy. "How on earth are you leaving your safe job for that crazy idea?" When she talked to her family and friends about the idea, they said she was crazy. She had always been independent, and now she was going to throw everything away to start working on that new idea. Most of her friends were not happy because she was now thinking differently. Why bother? But she was determined to change her life. She secretly had a plan, and the first step was to start working on that plan *now*.

So what was the next step? Who was the right person to ask for guidance? She started looking around for answers, but nothing seemed to click on her. She was an economist with an MBA, but she had worked in finance all her life. The options were getting a new job or starting her own business. But how to find a job in a bank or in a private equity firm? It did not resonate much, because it would be exchanging more money for time with herself and her family, and that was not ideal. The other option was to start a business, but doing what? She had no clue. She started thinking she was crazy. *Am I having a crisis of the forties? It could be, but I am determined to change what I don't like, if I can.*

The Plan and the Execution

The initial plan was to spend at least two hours per day lining up the plan by checking for options, searching online, and imagining herself doing different things. She also started testing some ideas she previously had when she was in her twenties. She realised that if she waited for everything to be perfect to start the plan, it might never happen.

Day by day she did something, even a little thing, to keep the pace—like setting up an online blog on her experience about being a working mum with kids, or selling clothing to full-time parents working from home or to people in the office who do not have much time. It sounded good. She started to set up a full plan with the best three options she got, and then she lined up the action plan.

Charlotte continued with two hours per day after work in the evenings to start the plan. It took around six months. She also took some online training because at the end of the day, between all the options she got, the most important thing she wanted was to have financial freedom to do whatever she wanted and help people fulfil their needs. Charlotte wanted more flexibility to enjoy her life and spend time with her kids, husband, and friends—and especially to take time to enjoy herself! That was something that she did not remember doing, at least in the last decade. On holidays, it was always rushing on a plane to stay somewhere for one or two weeks. Weekends were always full of activities with the kids, and sometimes she was working a couple of hours during the weekend. She called Mondays the resting day, where she had some time in the office to have a warm cup of tea. Charlotte was thinking about all those things, and she realised that every Monday, she was more tired than on Fridays after a long working week. She knew that her frenetic life had to change. She deserved this.

There was never time for anything. There was always something going on. When was the last time Charlotte had time to do a manicure and pedicure the whole morning without interruptions? Did she want to spend the next decade doing the same? No! It was the perfect incentive to continue working on her journey to freedom.

Charlotte started creating a company and lining up a plan regarding what to sell and how to sell it. She paid for some training to learn more about her new business. After a couple of weeks, Charlotte got very tired. Would she be able to cope with all those things? She had all her normal responsibilities, and on top of that, she was starting her own business. It was not easy at all. As the weeks passed, the idea was turning into a more shaped business. She was so proud of the advances. However, she started doubting whether all that effort was worth it. At the end of the day, she was working hard on that, but she was not sure it would work. Also, she could see that once the business launched, she would not have time to do all the things at the same time. Charlotte started checking when was the best time to leave her job. Could she survive? London was a very expensive city, and it is needed both her and her husband's salaries to survive there. She did not want to give up her life for a dream. What if it did not work?

Week after week, the hours spent in the new business increased more, and she could not afford to hire anyone to help her. Sometimes her daughters helped her, but it was not enough. She started doing some sales online, but it was not enough to quit her job. She had some savings, and she was waiting for her bonus at the beginning of next year. However, she knew if she wanted to succeed, there was a point where she would have to leave the safe path to achieve her dream. She did not want to throw away all the effort of the last six months. But she was so tired, and she saw some results, so she took the decision to leave her job. It was a difficult decision because the risk was huge.

Was that the right decision? Charlotte had no idea. However, there was something that made her take that step. At the end of the day, she had been working hard to create something from scratch that was already having results, though tiny. The question was when the right time was to leave her job.

A couple of weeks later, there was a situation that helped her make the decision. The right time was close. Charlotte received an email from her boss to apply for some training to help them develop their careers within the company. It was a leadership training with some of the directors of the company. There was a list of nice training that the employees could take to develop their careers and also meet some of the high-level directors of the company.

Charlotte was very excited about it. It could be a good opportunity to train herself in leadership. It would also help her entrepreneurial skills for her own company, and it might help her with her own career within the company. She chose one training that fitted with her job group classification in the company and would help her get the promotion she was expecting. It would help her have her last corporate job in a higher position while her own company was more stable.

She talked to her line manager, and the response was, "Sorry, but I think it doesn't fit you. We are looking for another type of person to apply for that training. Although you are in that job group, we need people with other skills." Charlotte felt very disappointing. She realised that her boss sent her the email simply to comply with the rules of sending it, but it was clear the person to do the training was already chosen—and it was not Charlotte. At the beginning, Charlotte felt angry and sad because she knew she could do it, but then she understood that in the end, it was a political decision, and someone else was chosen to take the training to help his or her career. And finally, it was the reason why she decided to leave the company. Why? Because it was clear that she would be in the same position for longer than expected, and her promotion might never happen. As Andrew had mentioned, if Charlotte stayed there, she would be there for years.

The options were stay there longer or make a move quickly. She had a notice period of three months and worked hard to have everything ready once she left the company. In addition, Charlotte was already working long hours between her full-time job and her business, and the time to choose one or another was getting closer.

Charlotte decided to resign. She did not sleep for a week. Something inside of her insisted that it was the right decision.

Charlotte left her safe, full-time job in February 2020 ... just before the COVID-19 pandemic started in the United Kingdom. She was very excited and felt free, but she worried because she had jumped into the unknown world. She had no idea that the craziest year of her life was ahead.

Charlotte walked away her former office. She handed her office badge to her now former boss and had contrary feelings. She was sad because it meant that she could no longer get into that building that had signified so much in the last seven years. Her boss simply turned back and came back to the building. Charlotte spent five minutes looking at the building and remembering all the good and bad moments she had had there: her first day there, when she got various promotions, and when she moved from one side to the building to the other side to meet new people. Now everything was over, and it was because of her own decision. She thought, *Did I make the right decision?* It was quite scary because she was used to being safe. However, she was determined to prove to herself that it was worth it. She turned away and walked to the tube with tears in her eyes.

After coming home, she thought she would like to have a magic ball to know that her decision was right. At the end of the day, she was the only one in charge of her destiny, but there were mortgage bills coming in every month, credit card bills, and two small children growing up. Her husband was at home waiting for her. It was a relief that he always supported her, but he was not happy with her decision. Now, without a job and as her own boss, she would have to figure out for herself what to do and how to do it. On that day, she started a long journey with a lot of ups and downs. It felt like opening the door to an amazing journey, and she was the driver!

PART II

THE ROLLER COASTER: THE REAL JOURNEY IS FINALLY HERE!

CHAPTER THREE

FREEDOM IS ON THE WAY

*C*HARLOTTE: *WELCOME TO reality! There is no way back now,* she thought as she started working full time on her business. Now she could spend 100 per cent of her time on it. In the last couple of months, she had worked for long hours between her full-time job and her new business. Charlotte went to bed late almost every day, and some days she barely slept three or four hours at night. It was sometimes too much work for her because she also had kids and housework to do. However, she could not afford to pay someone else yet. Although she had more time now, she was in a race against time to make her business profitable. She had only some savings to support her for the next six months.

The first day, she woke up early, and after the kids went to school, she started working on her business. It felt so good! She was now her own boss. By the time she left her full-time job, her business was six months old. She had some revenue, and she was comfortable with the mechanics of the business. However, the revenue was very small, so she was reliant on her savings, and now she did not have the income from her full-time job. Managing a business was a new skill for her, and she had to be very organised to make everything work. Her inspiration was to have the freedom to enjoy her life with her family and friends. She put a photo of her girls in front of her desk as a reminder of the reason why she wanted to succeed in her business! Charlotte knew that there was a long way until she reached what she wanted, but why not try? She remembered her conversation with Andrew, her ex-colleague. Charlotte knew that the first step to succeed was to start, test, adjust, and continue. If she waited for the right moment to start, it might never happen. Someone had said that done was better than perfect, and it resonated for many months in her head. Anyway, she would need that photo very much within the next year!

Charlotte was a business development director, but she had never had the experience of running her own online business. She had always worked for someone else. Now was the time to show to herself and to the world that she could make it happen! She was sourcing products from other countries to sell in the UK, working hard to make it happen quickly. However, she did not foresee something that would change the lives of millions of people around the world: COVID-19. A couple of weeks later, the lockdown started, and it would change the world forever.

COVID-19 Was on the Way!

Nobody could imagine a pandemic that would affect the whole world. It was unbelievable to think that everybody had to be at home and that everything would be closed to protect people from a virus. Well, yes, it was here, and Charlotte was starting a business during it. In addition, she had resigned to her job just a couple of weeks before. Someone would think that was the worst time to start a business. But there was no time for regrets; what was done, was done. Now, the only way was to continue with her project and adjust it under the new circumstances.

Charlotte's business was an online business, importing clothes and toys from China and other parts of Europe to sell them in the UK. By the time she had resigned, the store was already selling a decent number of items, mainly baby and women's clothing. She also used Amazon to sell online. Between both income streams, for six to twelve months she should be able to live from her savings, and with the right investment, in one year she should be able to have a decent business. However, under the new pandemic circumstances, it was clearly challenging for her, especially the first months when the government closed the borders in the UK to avoid transmission between people. It meant that some of her products never arrived. In addition, she was selling online clothes for working woman and stuff for babies and kids. The business clearly did not go well, and she lost a lot of money between additional fees to import the items and the increase of the price of the items she was selling online. In addition, during the lockdown, nobody was buying dresses to go to the office, or nappy bags! Clearly it was not the market for the COVID-19 year. That year was difficult because she also had limited funds; she still had to pay bills at home. Her full-time job salary was not there, and the kids were full time at home for schooling.

It was a difficult time for many middle-class families, and Charlotte's was not an exception.

What were the options? On one hand, it was not that bad because she had never spent so much time with her kids and her husband, because she always had worked full time, and her husband had always worked long hours as well. It was like meeting someone who was always there, but you did not know them. On the other hand, it was challenging because she did not have the income she used to have, and even if they were at home, the bills had to be paid month by month. April, May, June—all those months passed, and her business was worse than when she had left her job. Some days she did not sleep because she could not see the light at the end of the tunnel. But did she want to go back to her job? She asked herself many times, and the response was no. She thought that if she sought a new job, there was nothing happening in the market, so it would be difficult to find something. Or she could continue with her project and try to get a loan to fund the business. She had to change the strategy.

Every single day when she woke up, she reminded herself that it was a new day, and that helped her focus on what mattered. She asked herself if it was a good decision to leave her previous job, however she always reached the same conclusion:

It was what it was, and she had made the decision based on the information she had had at that moment. Nobody could foresee that crazy situation of a pandemic. Because she was self-employed without other income and with a lot of debt, it was difficult to get loans in the market at an affordable rate. After many loan applications, finally she got a loan that allowed her to start again from scratch. It was already August, and the first lockdown in England had ended in July 2020, so the economy was recovering very slowly. She had to change her business because it was unclear when people would come back to the offices, and the market for office clothing was dead. Most of her products for babies where not that appealing to the market anymore because apart from basic things, people were cautious to buy like they had before the pandemic. She decided to change her target market and started selling groceries online. It went better, but by the time she started to have some profit, she ran out of money. Her savings were gone, and it was almost January 2021.

The third lockdown started. At that point it was difficult to source the business because only supermarkets were open, and getting any loan to invest was very expensive because her credit rating was poor at that moment. What to do? Her idea was to find a consultancy job a couple of days per week to have time to fund the business and work on that. The kids were back to school in May 2021, so she could have time again to work on her business. Fortunately, that year passed fast, and she had time to think about her future and what she really wanted. She had an amazing year with her girls and husband, and she was lucky because her sisters and mother lived very close to her. She knew that having a job was safe, but it was an exchange for her time and freedom. With a job, Charlotte would be safe until she got retired, but her earnings had a cap. With a business, it was more challenging, and the safety of income was not there, at least at the beginning. She realised that entrepreneurs had to be resilient and have a positive mindset because every single day was a challenge with ups and downs. Charlotte wished she had a crystal ball to know what would happen in the future. Would she succeed? She had no idea. However, she was trying her best. If she did not succeed, at least she knew she had tried. However, if she did succeed, it would be amazing. And again she thought to herself, *Why not try?*

Finding Another Source of Income

May 2021 finally arrived. Charlotte was very happy because she had found a flexible job that allowed her to continue with the business. Again it was challenging because now she had a job and had to optimise her time on her business, keeping a decent balance with her family life. Did she have any other option? Not really!

The months passed quickly. Charlotte worked day and night. She was happy in her new job because it was very similar to her previous one, and she liked what she did. After COVID-19, it was clear that the world she knew before the pandemic was different. Everything was online. Work trips were deleted from the vocabulary, and her colleagues were more relaxed working from home. It was the perfect atmosphere to enjoy her new life, and because Charlotte was working from home, she could better organise her time between her business and her job. Without commuting, it made her life a lot easier. The business started growing back again because now she had some money to invest in it. It was hard work, but it was worth it. She still had the picture of her daughters in front of her desk, and it was her incentive to continue with her business.

The end of the year arrived, and there were so many things happening. Charlotte was very excited because her business was growing so much. She could not believe all the things that had happened in her personal and professional life during those two years. It was good that although everything seemed to be against her decision to start a business, perseverance worked out in the end.

She had so many sleepless nights, and sometimes the job crashed with her business, but at the end of the day, everything worked out perfectly. She learned that believing in your dreams and reaching for them always pays. What a wonderful example for her daughters. Her business was going well. Her job was going well as well, but this time she decided to think twice before leaving the job until she had secured a proper flow of money. She wanted to reinvest all the income back to the business.

Reflecting on what she had done, she was proud of herself that she had made the decision to leave her previous safe job because she was not happy there. She knew that in that safe job, nobody would fire her, but she would not progress either.

If she had not left her job when she had, she probably would still have been there, in the same job with the same people and doing the same things every day. At the end of the day, it took a lot of courage to decide to move outside her comfort zone. Of course, it was not an easy decision.

The action plan had been decided. Now that the business was growing slowly but surely and she had a new flexible job, she could continue with her business plan. Charlotte designed a timeline to leave her current job in a couple of years. She was glad that she had never given up, even in the worst circumstances. In addition, she learned new skills, and she was able to build a sustainable business during the COVID-19 pandemic. If she was able to survive that chaotic year, she knew she would be able to succeed. It seemed that the worst was behind her.

CHAPTER FOUR

DEVELOPING THE PLAN—AGAIN

CHARLOTTE WAS FINANCIALLY stable, she received a fixed monthly income, and the business growing slowly but steadily. She could finally continue with her plans. With the experience she had gained in the last six months, knowing what to do and what not to do, she fine-tuned her plan. The first thing she did was hire someone to help her in about four months. Charlotte would continue with her current job until she reached a monthly income that was enough to cover all her expenses, including leaving some money to reinvest back into the business. According to her numbers, it would be around three years. There was a long journey ahead, but this time was different because this time, she knew what to do. It was different than the first time, when she had started but had no clue what she was doing. Now she had more than a year of experience, and things were starting to be shaped for the future.

Her basic income was sorted to cover the bills, and things were flowing with less stress than before. She could plan her next moves at least a month in advance. The economy was back to the new normal, most people were vaccinated in the UK, and there was a positive environment around the economy. After all, the previous year had been emotionally and economically difficult for so many families, so a fresh start was a great thing. It was scary for her but was also a great lesson for her life. Never, never give up because there is always a way to find a way to make it work, even if it means changing the plan almost completely.

Charlotte's business was divided in two streams. One was her online business at Amazon, and the second was creating her own website, which was the original idea, but now she was sourcing the business with more local products from different sources. The combination of Brexit and COVID-19 had been challenging for a lot of businesses, and a new era with more online competitors was starting, with a very different market than before 2019. It was challenging, but Charlotte enjoyed it. She was glad that she had made the decision to leave her job and embark on this new, crazy idea. Now she had the experience and learning she did not have before, and she knew it was her chance to find financial freedom for her and her family.

After a couple of weeks working hard between her job and her business, and juggling between children and work, she realised that she needed more money to grow her business, otherwise the pace to grow would take longer than she wanted. At the end of each month, the money left to invest in her business after paying bills and debt was very small, leaving no room for her business to grow.

She went to the market to get loans for her business, but because she had so much debt, was the sole owner of her business, and had a credit rating that was not great, the loans available were too expensive. She looked for grants or any other facilities, but it was difficult because her business was too new without enough trading experience. In addition, she would need at least two years more of trading to get an affordable rate, and with the fact that she had already gotten a loan at the beginning of the pandemic, the loan options were challenging. Maybe she would find some equity, or she might get a loan from friends or family.

According to Charlotte's numbers, she needed at least ten thousand pounds to really ramp up her business. She knew exactly how to invest that money to get the expected results. Now the task was to get those additional ten thousand.

Where would she find the funds? Charlotte decided to check with a bank now that she had a job and was up to date with all the payments. The situation was different now. Last time she had gotten ten rejections for loans because she was a self-employee and her company had less than three years trading in the market. Now, her company was still younger than three years, but she was not self-employed anymore. She had a job, and it might help her now.

She spent one whole day searching for loans. Some of

the loan rates were so crazy that she wondered how on earth someone could pay them. *You must be crazy to apply for those loans.* Sometimes lenders take advantage of the credit rating record to increase the rates to unbearable levels to lend to desperate people, arguing that the risk is too high. It should be regulated! However, she found two lenders at an affordable rate, and she decided to apply for the loans and send all the information requested. It took a couple of days to hear from them. At the end of the week, an underwriter called her, and later that day, one of them approved her for a loan! It was the best moment ever. She finally could grow her business!

With the funds to begin investing again, she found new products to test on a bigger scale. Now she had more than one year of experience trading in the market, and she kind of knew what worked and what did not work. She perfected her initial strategy, looking at products that gave her a good margin and were easy to sell. With more experience, she learned more about her business. She found new suppliers, and some of her products sold very well. Month after month, she saw that her business was growing, and she reinvested the income back into the business. She started planning the new season in advance. In that way, she had more negotiation margin to get better prices, buying more products and learning more about the market for the big season: December.

Every week there was a lot of work, but Charlotte enjoyed it. The summer and autumn were over, and winter was coming. Her products were selling well, and she found some new products that her customers loved. She was reinvesting the money month after month. By the end of November, she had recovered half of the initial investment. The competition was fierce, and some days she had bad days, but many days were fine. Sometimes it looked like a long road, and her working hours were long as well. However, Charlotte's attitude was positive most of the time. The picture on her desk with her daughters was the best incentive to reach her goals, and Charlotte was determined to have financial freedom. She would not give up.

Finally December arrived. There were so many expectations regarding the Christmas sales. She had been preparing for the last six months to double her monthly sales in that month. It was so exciting. Looking back at her journey up to now was crazy. It had been a roller coaster. That month went smoothly, she sold a lot, and she finally doubled the sales. She reached one thousand pounds per day!

When she had created the company in September 2019, she thought that the goal of selling one thousand per day would be very easy. She thought she was prepared and that it would take six to twelve months. She took some training that was very useful, but the real learning was doing it hands-on and learning on the way of things. If she had given up when she had run out of money, she would not have known whether she would be able to reach her dream of selling one thousand pounds per day. Sometimes it is easier to give up than take the long journey, learning and adjusting until reaching one's goals. Every single day was different.

Charlotte was proud of herself. She cried of happiness. She gave a big hug to her daughters, her husband, and her family.

She knew everything was worth it, and there was no going back now. She realised that she was a different person than when she had started her business. She had persevered until she made it. She understood that in most cases, being afraid stopped her from making decisions, but she was glad she had taken the first step, and that the new step brought another step. She continued until she was where she was now. It was an amazing moment.

CHAPTER FIVE

HAVING A SUSTAINABLE BUSINESS

Now What?

JANUARY HAD ARRIVED again. Charlotte was happy with her holiday results. However, she did not realise that it was the beginning of the real journey. Do you know that building a profitable business is not enough if the business can't survive the first years in a sustainable way? Building a viable business was the challenge now. Her refurbished plan from the past year was a three-year plan that included keeping her full-time job for at least a couple of years until she had more than enough income to depend solely on her business.

The first year of her refurbished plan was on, and she already had results. However, it was not enough because the sales were not stable yet. In January, the sales dropped to half, and the excitement of December was quickly replaced with the design of a new strategy for the following months of less demand. She had planned most of the previous year based on the Christmas sales, but what about January, February, and March?

She needed to adjust her strategy for those months—again. Every single season is different in terms of sales, and a different strategy is needed for each season. However, Charlotte had been so focused on December's sales that she almost forgot about the first quarter of the next year.

To make a long story short, she started buying new products for the following seasons with a lot of products in clearance, but she also started thinking about the new steps for her business. She had the idea of hiring someone to help her with the business. She hired one person to help her grow the business, mainly to help her pack and get new products to sell.

She also had a lot of inventory trapped in her house. It was so much that her house looked like a warehouse, and her husband was not very happy about it. Therefore, she leased a place to take and organise the excess inventory close to her house, and it was affordable for the business.

With her new team and the new place, she already had the tools to better plan for the current year and buy more inventory in advance now that she had a place to store it. Costs were always a very important part of a long-term sustainable business, and she knew that cash was king.

Her full-time job was also going well because it was in something where she had decades of experience, however it was clear that it would not be a long-term occupation, because her business was growing, and she knew that it would be her future. Charlotte knew that after so many years of her experience working all around the world, she was ready to move on to her new passion: her own business. However, she was also aware that the business was not ready yet to give her the final jump to a full-time entrepreneur. It required time and effort to continue with her lifestyle whilst starting a company and working in a job, plus having a family. The effort was totally worth it, and it would not be forever.

Time passed very fast that year. Charlotte was very busy trying to achieve the expected results. By the time April passed, she finally had a sustainable number of sales per day. Being an entrepreneur and having employees was huge because she must make ends meet at the month's end to pay salaries, accountants, and sometimes lawyers. The most important thing was to manage people to keep them inspired and happy in their jobs. By the time the summer ended, she had a team of five people working in the company. She was glad that everything was going well, and it was amazing to know that she was providing money to five different families.

Two years passed, with hard work and ups and downs. The business was growing, and more employees joined the company. Charlotte sometimes could not believe that her tenacity and her decision to move outside her comfort zone could end in a great business. Of course it was not easy at all, and it took time, and there were still a lot of things to do. Finally, she could leave her job to be a 100 per cent entrepreneur.

Things were not always as planned, but in general they

worked out as expected. Now she could spend more time with her business, she had financial freedom to spend more time with her family, and she was earning more than in any job she had dreamed of.

It was soon more than five years since the September she had decided to start her company. Something that she had thought would take a couple of years became more than five years of working hard. Many times she had to start from scratch, but the most important thing was that she never gave up. She believed in herself, and she succeeded. She knew that starting and never giving up, even during the ups and downs, were the most difficult parts of entrepreneurship. For some others, it is easier to drop everything and continue with the easy path. It was not Charlotte's case. Her tenacity and perseverance finally paid off.

Charlotte was happy because she was an example for her daughters, her family, and her closest friends.

Dreams Are Real!

Finally, she had done it! Everything was possible. Now she could enjoy her dream coming true of having her own successful business, as well as having the freedom to choose what to do, with whom, when, and how. She asked herself, *Why did I not start earlier?* Because she had thought that being successful was only for other people, the lucky people—not her. She was afraid that she would be one of the many people who failed. She understood that her success was not a lucky event. It was the result of hard work, perseverance, and constant adjustment to new circumstances. However, the most important factor was to believe in herself and never give up. Even in the harshest circumstances like starting a business during the pandemic, she could succeed.

Her life was exciting, she really enjoyed her journey to freedom, and she had many plans in the future. She was not a modern slave anymore. She was free!

CONCLUSION

Charlotte was a successful, professional worker who had a perfect life. It could be 90 per cent of the population. She was blessed because she lived in London with a loving family. She had worked hard to reach her position, but there was something missing. This was a situation that many employees face during their working life. After different situations, she had the courage to starting something completely new and change her life because she did not feel complete. Fear was always there, but even so, she took the first step, which is often the most difficult step.

Sometimes we spend all our lives waiting for the "right" moment to start something, and then it is too late because the conditions were never perfect. In this case, Charlotte realised that it was better to start now than wait for the "right" moment. Fear was quite often the worst adviser, so why not try now? If she did not do it, she would never know what would happen.

Starting a new business is always challenging. The most common belief is that having a job is a safe option, but it does not guarantee safety, and in most cases the income is capped independent of the worked hours or how efficient the employeeis. Charlotte saw her future self in her colleague Andrew. It might happen to her if she continued working in that company. Every day, she saw how other colleagues spent their lives working from nine to five until they retired. Perhaps for our parents, having a full-time job was the safest option. However, that might not be the same today. Especially after the recent recessions and the pandemic, it is hard to say that all jobs are safe. So why not try?

For Charlotte, it was important to find another source of income while she was still trying, and it was the right option. But even after she found a second job, she never changed her goal. Reaching your dreams requires tenacity and a clear goal. Charlotte wanted financial freedom to enjoy her family and her life. It took some years, but she never gave up. Also, her mindset helped her a lot. Even during a crisis, it is important to be optimistic because there is always a way to reach one's goals. When Charlotte ran out of money, she looked for a job and got a new loan to grow her business, always adjusting to new situations.

Another important aspect to highlight is that she always believed in herself, and she took some courses to help her hone her new skills. She kept trying and adjusting the plan despite the odds that she faced during her journey. In addition, there are always people around who will try to minimise the work done to persuade entrepreneurs like Charlotte to drop their plans, saying that it is impossible. The key is having a clear mindset and clear goals. There are thousands of examples of companies that fail, but it does not mean that it will be your case.

Her journey had a lot of ups and downs, but in the end she succeeded. Maybe the next entrepreneur is you. Why not try?

Final Thoughts

1. You do not need to have a winner idea to start a business, because at the end of the day, the only way to know whether or not a business is successful is through trial and error. Sometimes the initial idea has nothing to do with the final successful idea.

2. Many people give up at the first try. Having a successful business does not have anything to do with luck. Successful businesspeople are the ones who never give up.

3. Starting is the most difficult part to creating a business. You do not need to be a super intelligent person or someone who takes tons of risks. Most successful businesspeople are the ones who step out of their comfort zone. It is a panicking situation for 99 per cent of entrepreneurs, but they are the only ones who confront their fears to make a difference in their lives, working hard to make it happen and changing and improving their own businesses until they find the solutions needed in their market niche.

4. The only way to find out whether you are good at something is to try it.

5. It is wrong to think that you need to leave your job to start a business. Cash flow is key. Leave your job only when you know that you can live from your business without compromising your own business growth.

6. Do you have the excuse of "I don't have time"? That is just an excuse! Stop watching Netflix and social media! You need only two to three hours per week consistently to start a business.

7. Another typical excuse is, "I have kids, so I don't have time." Charlotte was working full time and had two kids. There are a lot of entrepreneurs who are parents, and they build their own successful businesses while having children.

8. You don't need to pay hundreds of pounds to train yourself to learn something. There are a lot of cheap or free online courses on the Internet that teach you how to properly start a business. Do not fall into the trap of paying thousands of pounds for training. Always check the reviews online from a trusted site. If there are no reviews, then it is suspicious. Some of the best courses are the ones that give a lot of free treats and have online tribes to share experiences for free. If you do not find reviews, think twice about investing in that training.

9. If you want to exit your nine-to-five Job life safely, bear in mind that it is a process that takes time and effort. You need to first learn how to do it, practicing so you know what works and what doesn't. With a consistent practice and a testing/error/adjusting/testing

approach, it might take time, and you might lose some money, but you will learn from that experience pain-free. However, persistence and consistency are the key factor for success. Test with small amounts of money first, and test, test, and test until it works. Do not risk big amounts of money if you cannot afford it; start with a small investment that you wouldn't mind losing. You can always start testing your ideas with family and friends before moving on to other people.

10. You do not need to be an expert in anything special to start a business. Start trying something online with low risk and a low investment during your spare time, and check how it goes. You can even start selling things you do not use at home. There are online training courses at an affordable price to teach you new skills, like Jim Cokrum's course on selling in Amazon. He wrote *Silent Sales Machine*.

11. Whether or not you have a clear business not, always create a simple business plan. There are plenty of business plans online. They will give you a framework of what to do, how to do it, and when to do it. Numbers are important. Run some high-level numbers to know how much money you need.

12. Listen to your intuition. There are a lot of naysayers around. Believe in your gut feelings and always believe in yourself. If it goes wrong the first or the second time, it doesn't mean that the third time is going to be wrong as well. If you have failed, you have learned what

does not work—congratulations! There is always a new opportunity available for you, so why not try again? Remember that every day is a new day with fresh, new air. Try again and don't give up.

13. The most important thing is to start today! Procrastination and fear are the worst advisors for anything. Make no excuses. You can be free, but it depends on you! Nobody is going to do it for you. Why not try?

BIBLIOGRAPHY

Cantwell, Marianne. (2013). *Be a Free Range Human: Escape the 9–5, Create a Life You Love, and Still Pay the Bills*. London: Kogan Page.

Cockrum, J. 2014. *Silent Sales Machine 10.0.*: Servus.

Ferris, T. 2011. *The 4-Hour Workweek: Escape 9–5, Live Anywhere, and Join the New Rich*. New York: Vermilion.

Kiyosaki, R., and S. Lechter. 1997. *Rich Dad, Poor Dad*. Scottsdale, AZ: Plata.

Tracy, B. 2004. *Eat That Frog! Get More of the Important Things Done—Today!* London: Hodder & Stoughton.

"ACKNOWLEDGMENTS"

I would like to thank my husband for being my biggest supporter. To my daughters for being my biggest strength. To my two sisters, mum, dad, Juan, Francesca, and Olivia for being always there for me.

ABOUT THE AUTHOR

Carolina is a writer, entrepreneur, and businesswoman. She has an MBA (Hons) in Economics. She lives in London, is married, and is the mother of two daughters.

She is part of the board of directors of various UK companies.

She has more than fifteen years of experience in the energy sector. She is an expert in origination, business development, and more.

She is a business coach at www.carolinacanosacriado.com helping thousands of people to set up their own businesses.

She is owner of Stork Market, an online store: www.stork-market-ltd.myshopify.com.